Astronomy

What is the biblical perspective?

A POCKET GUIDE TO . . .

Astronomy

What is the biblical perspective?

Petersburg, Kentucky, USA

Reprinted September 2014

ISBN: 1-60092-302-X

Printed in China

answersingenesis.org

Table of Contents

Introduction

The universe is so large that we really can't understand its immensity. No one can look at the stars on a clear night and not be in awe. The focus of that awe is different for various groups of people. Some look at the universe as the result of a cosmic explosion in which random arangements of atoms have resulted in the beauty displayed in galaxies and nebulae.

Others look at the universe and understand it to be a result of the intentional design of God. Rather than random arrangements, the heavens declare the glory of God. Many passages in Scripture give God the glory for the works of creation.

The ideas put forward by proponents of the big bang are in direct opposition to the ideas set forward in the Bible. Although astronomy can seem intimidating to many, the articles in this book will help you to understand the distinction between a naturalistic universe and one that is the result of a mighty Creator God.

Does the Bible Say Anything about Astronomy?

by Jason Lisle

The Bible is the history book of the universe. It tells us how the universe began and how it came to be the way it is today.

The Bible is much more than just a history book, however; it was written by inspiration of God. The Lord certainly understands how this universe works; after all, He made it. So His Word, the Bible, gives us the foundation for understanding the universe.

It has been said that the Bible is not a science textbook. This is true, of course, and it's actually a good thing. After all, our science textbooks are based on the ideas of human beings who do not know everything and who often make mistakes. That's why science textbooks change from time to time, as people discover new evidence and realize that they were wrong about certain things.

The Bible, though, never changes because it never needs to. God got it right the first time! The Bible is the infallible Word of God. So when it touches on a particular topic, it's right. When the Bible talks about geology, it's correct. When Scripture addresses biology or anthropology, it's also right.

What does the Bible teach about astronomy? Let's take a look at some of the things the Bible has to say about the universe. We will see that the Bible is absolutely correct when it deals with astronomy.

The earth is round

The Bible indicates that the earth is round. One verse we can look at is Isaiah 40:22, where it mentions the "circle of the earth." From space, the earth always appears as a circle since it is round. This matches perfectly with the Bible.

Another verse to consider is Job 26:10, where it teaches that God has "inscribed" a circle on the surface of the waters at the boundary of light and darkness. This boundary between light and darkness is where evening and morning occur. The boundary is a circle since the earth is round.

The earth floats in space

A very interesting verse to consider is Job 26:7, which states that God "hangs the earth on nothing." This might make you think of God hanging the earth like a Christmas tree ornament, but hanging it on empty space. Although this verse is written in a poetic way, it certainly seems to suggest that the earth floats in space; and indeed the earth does float in space. We now have pictures of the earth taken from space that show it floating in the cosmic void. The earth literally hangs upon nothing, just as the Bible suggests.

- The Hindus believed the earth to be supported on the backs of four elephants, which stand on the shell of a gigantic tortoise floating on the surface of the world's waters.

- The earth of the Vedic priests was set on 12 solid pillars; its upper side was its only habitable side.

- The Altaic people of Northern Siberia affirm that their mighty Ulgen created the earth on the waters and placed under it three great fish to support it.

- The Tartars and many of the other tribes of Eurasia believed the earth to be supported by a great bull.

The expansion of the universe

The Bible indicates in several places that the universe has been "stretched out" or expanded. For example, Isaiah 40:22 teaches that God stretches out the heavens like a curtain and spreads them out like a tent to dwell in. This would suggest that the universe has actually increased in size since its creation. God is stretching it out, causing it to expand.

Now, this verse must have seemed very strange when it was first written. The universe certainly doesn't look as if it is expanding. After all, if you look at the night sky tonight, it will appear about the same size as it did the previous night, and the night before that.

In fact, secular scientists once believed that the universe was eternal and unchanging. The idea of an expanding universe would have been considered nonsense to most scientists of the past. So it must have been tempting for Christians to reject what the Bible teaches about the expansion of the universe.

I wonder if any Christians tried to "reinterpret" Isaiah 40:22 to read it in an unnatural way so that they wouldn't have to believe in an expanding universe. When the secular world believes one thing and the Bible teaches another, it is always tempting to think that God got the details wrong. But God is never wrong.

Most astronomers today believe that the universe is indeed expanding. In the 1920s, astronomers discovered that virtually all clusters of galaxies appear to be moving away from all other clusters; this indicates that the entire universe is expanding.

You can think of this like points on a balloon. As the balloon is inflated, all the points move farther away from each other. If the entire universe was being stretched out, the galaxies would all be moving away; and that is what they actually appear to be doing.

It is fascinating that the Bible recorded the idea of an expanding universe thousands of years before secular science came to accept the idea.

The age of the universe

Scripture also addresses the age of the universe. The Bible teaches that the entire universe was created in six days (Exodus 20:11). We know from the genealogies and other events recorded in Scripture that this creation happened about 6,000 years ago.

Yet, this is quite different from what most schools teach. Most secular scientists believe that the universe is many billions of years old and they usually hold to the big bang theory. The big bang is a secular speculation about the origin of the universe; it is an alternative to the Bible's teaching. The big bang attempts to explain the origin of the universe without God (see the next chapter, "Does the big bang fit with the Bible?").

People who believe in the big bang usually interpret the evidence according to their already-existing belief in the big bang. In other words, they just assume that the big bang is true; they interpret the evidence to match their beliefs. Of course, the Bible can also be used to interpret the evidence. And since the Bible records the true history of the universe, we see that it makes a lot more sense of the evidence than the big bang does.

Now let's look at some facts about the universe regarding its age. We will see that the evidence is consistent with 6,000 years but doesn't make sense if we hold to the big bang.

Of course, big bang supporters can always reinterpret the evidence by adding extra assumptions. So, the following facts are not intended to "prove" that the Bible is right about the age of the universe. The Bible is right in all matters because it is the Word of God. However, when we understand the scientific evidence, we will find that it agrees with what the Bible teaches. The evidence is certainly consistent with a young universe.

Recession of the moon

The moon is slowly moving away from the earth. As the moon orbits the earth, its gravity pulls on the earth's oceans, which causes tides. The tides actually "pull forward" on the moon, causing the moon to gradually spiral outward. So the moon moves about an inch and a half away from the earth every year. That means that the moon would have been closer to the earth in the past.

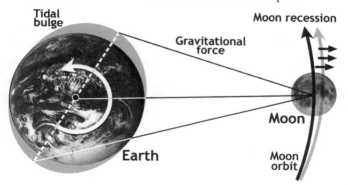

For example, six thousand years ago, the moon would have been about 800 feet closer to the earth (which is not much of a change, considering the moon is a quarter of a million miles away). So this "spiraling away" of the moon is not a problem over the biblical timescale of 6,000 years. But if the earth and moon were over four billion years old (as evolutionists teach), then we would have big problems. In this case, the moon would have been so close that it would actually have been touching the earth only 1.4 billion years ago. This problem suggests that the moon can't possibly be as old as secular astronomers claim.

Secular astronomers who assume that the big bang is true must use other explanations to get around this. For example, they might assume that the rate at which the moon was receding was actually smaller in the past. But this is an extra assumption needed to make their billions-of-years model work. The simplest explanation is that the moon hasn't been around for that long. The recession of the moon is a problem for a belief in billions of years but is perfectly consistent with a young age.

Magnetic fields of the planets

Many of the planets of the solar system have strong magnetic fields. These fields are caused by electrical currents that decay with time. We can even measure this decay of the earth's magnetic field: it gets weaker and weaker every year. If the planets were really billions of years old (as evolutionists believe) then their magnetic fields should be extremely weak by now. Yet they are not. The outer planets of the solar system, in particular, have quite strong magnetic fields. A reasonable explanation for this is that these planets are only a few thousand years old, as the Bible teaches.

Spiral galaxies

A galaxy is an enormous assembly of stars, interstellar gas and dust. The galaxy in which we live is called the Milky Way; it has over 100 billion stars. Some galaxies are round or elliptical. Others have an irregular shape, but some of the most beautiful galaxies are spiral in nature, such as our own. Spiral galaxies slowly rotate, but the inner regions of the spiral rotate faster than the outer regions. This means that a spiral galaxy is constantly becoming more and more twisted up as the spiral becomes tighter. After a few hundred million years, the galaxy would be wound so tightly that the spiral structure would no longer be recognizable. According to the big bang scenario, galaxies are supposed to be many billions of years

NASA/ESA

old. Yet we do see spiral galaxies—and lots of them. This suggests that they are not nearly as old as the big bang requires. Spiral galaxies are consistent with the biblical age of the universe but are problematic for a belief in billions of years.

Comets

Comets are balls of ice and dirt. Many of them orbit the sun in elliptical paths. They spend most of their time far away from the sun, but occasionally they come very close to it. Every time a comet comes near the sun, some of its icy material is blasted away by the solar radiation. As a result, comets can orbit the sun for only so long (perhaps about 100,000 years at most) before they completely run out of material. Since we still have a lot of comets, this suggests that the solar system is much younger than 100,000 years; this agrees perfectly with the Bible's history.

Yet, secular astronomers believe the solar system is 4.5 billion years old. Since comets can't last that long, secular astronomers must assume that new comets are created to replace those that are gone. So they've invented the idea of an "Oort cloud." This is supposed to be a vast reservoir of icy masses orbiting far away from the sun. The idea is that occasionally an icy mass falls into the inner solar system to become a "new" comet. It is interesting that there is currently no evidence of an Oort cloud. And there's no reason to believe in one if we accept the creation account in Genesis. Comets are consistent with the fact that the solar system is young.

Supernatural creation

Aside from age, there are other indications that the universe was supernaturally created as the Bible teaches. These evidences show God's creativity—not a big bang. For example, astronomers have discovered "extrasolar" planets. These are planets that orbit distant stars—not our sun. These planets have not been directly observed. Instead, they have been detected indirectly—usually by the gravitational "tug" they produce on the star they orbit. But the principles being used here are all good "operational science"—the kind of testable, repeatable science that can be done in a laboratory. So we have every reason to believe that these are indeed real planets that God created.

These extrasolar planets are actually a problem for big-bang, evolutionary models of solar system formation. Secular astronomers had expected that other solar systems would resemble ours—with small planets forming very closely to their star and large planets (like Jupiter and Saturn) forming farther away. But many of these extrasolar planets are just the opposite; they are large Jupiter-sized planets orbiting very closely to their star. This is inconsistent with evolutionary models of solar system formation, but it's not a problem for biblical creation. God can create many different varieties of solar systems, and apparently He has done just that.

Conclusion

We have seen that when the Bible addresses the topic of astronomy, it is accurate in every aspect. This shouldn't be surprising because the Bible, which teaches that the heavens declare the glory and handiwork of God (Psalm 19:1), is the written Word of the Creator. God understands every aspect of the universe He has created, and He never makes mistakes.

In addition, the Word of God provides the correct foundation for understanding the scientific evidence. At the same time, the Bible provides more than just information on the physical universe. It also answers the most profound questions of life. Why are we here? How should we live? And what happens when we die? The Word of God even answers the question of why there is death and suffering in the world.[1]

We can have confidence that what the Bible says about our need for salvation is true, because the Bible has demonstrated itself to be accurate time after time. Showing our children how true science confirms the Bible will help them answer the evolutionary attacks they encounter at schools and in the media.

---

1.   See www.AnswersInGenesis.org/go/curse.

 **Dr. Jason Lisle** holds a PhD in astrophysics from the University of Colorado at Boulder. Dr. Lisle is a popular author and speaker on the topics of creation and apologetics. He is currently the Director of Research at the Institute for Creation Research.

Does the Big Bang Fit with the Bible?

by Jason Lisle

The "big bang" is a story about how the universe came into existence. It proposes that billions of years ago the universe began in a tiny, infinitely hot and dense point called a singularity. This singularity supposedly contained not only all the mass and energy that would become everything we see today, but also "space" itself. According to the story, the singularity rapidly expanded, spreading out the energy and space.

It is supposed that over vast periods of time, the energy from the big bang cooled down as the universe expanded. Some of it turned into matter—hydrogen and helium gas. These gases collapsed to form stars and galaxies of stars. Some of the stars created

the heavier elements in their core and then exploded, distributing these elements into space. Some of the heavier elements allegedly began to stick together and formed the earth and other planets.

This story of origins is entirely fiction. But sadly, many people claim to believe the big bang model. It is particularly distressing that many professing Christians have been taken in by the big bang, perhaps without realizing its atheistic underpinnings. They have chosen to reinterpret the plain teachings of Scripture in an attempt to make it mesh with secular beliefs about origins.

Secular compromises

There are several reasons why we cannot just add the big bang to the Bible. Ultimately, the big bang is a *secular* story of origins. When first proposed, it was an attempt to explain how the universe could have been created without God. Really, it is an *alternative* to the Bible; so it makes no sense to try to "add" it to the

Secular view

Big Bang	Stars	Sun	Molten Earth	First oceans
15 Billion years ago	10 Billion years ago	5 Billion years ago	4.5 Billion years ago	3.8 Billion years ago

Biblical view

Water covered Earth	Dry land and plants	Sun, moon and stars	Sea and flying creatures	Land animals and man
Day 1-2	Day 3	Day 4	Day 5	Day 6

Bible. Let us examine some of the profound differences between the Bible and the secular big bang view of origins.

The Bible teaches that God created the universe in six days (Genesis 1; Exodus 20:11). It is clear from the context in Genesis that these were days in the ordinary sense (i.e., 24-hour days) since they are bounded by evening and morning and occur in an ordered list (second day, third day, etc.). Conversely, the big bang teaches the universe has evolved over billions of years.

The Bible says that Earth was created before the stars and that trees were created before the sun.[1] However, the big bang view teaches the exact opposite. The Bible tells us that the earth was created as a paradise; the secular model teaches it was created as a molten blob. The big bang and the Bible certainly do not agree about the past.

Many people don't realize that the big bang is a story not only about the past but also about the future. The most popular version of the big bang teaches that the universe will expand forever and eventually run out of usable energy. According to the story, it

will remain that way forever in a state that astronomers call "heat death."[2] But the Bible teaches that the world will be judged and remade. Paradise will be restored. The big bang denies this crucial biblical teaching.

Scientific problems with the big bang

The big bang also has a number of scientific problems. Big bang supporters are forced to accept on "blind faith" a number of notions that are completely *inconsistent* with real observational science. Let's explore some of the inconsistencies between the big bang story and the real universe.

Missing monopoles

Most people know something about magnets—like the kind found in a compass or the kind that sticks to a refrigerator. We often say that magnets have two "poles"—a north pole and a south pole. Poles that are alike will repel each other, while opposites attract. A "monopole" is a hypothetical massive particle that is just like a magnet but has only one pole. So a monopole would have either a north pole or a south pole, but not both.

Particle physicists claim that many magnetic monopoles should have been created in the high temperature conditions of the big bang. Since monopoles are stable, they should have lasted to this day. Yet, despite considerable search efforts, monopoles have not been found. Where are the monopoles? The fact that we don't find any monopoles suggests that the universe never was that hot. This indicates that there never was a big bang, but it is perfectly consistent with the Bible's account of creation, since the universe did not start infinitely hot.

The flatness problem

Another serious challenge to the big bang model is called the "flatness problem." The expansion rate of the universe appears to be very finely balanced with the force of gravity; this condition is called "flat." If the universe were the accidental byproduct of a big bang, it is difficult to imagine how such a fantastic coincidence could occur. Big bang cosmology cannot explain why the matter density in the universe isn't greater, causing it to collapse upon itself (closed universe), or less, causing the universe to rapidly fly apart (open universe).

The problem is even more severe when we extrapolate into the past. Since any deviation from perfect flatness tends to increase as time moves forward, it logically follows that the universe must have been *even more* precisely balanced in the past than it is today. Thus, at the moment of the big bang, the universe would have been virtually flat to an extremely high precision. This must have been the case (assuming the big bang), despite the fact that the laws of physics allow for an *infinite* range of values. This is a coincidence that stretches credulity to the breaking point. Of course, in the creation model, "balance" is expected since the Lord has fine-tuned the universe for life.

Inflating the complexities

Many secular astronomers have come up with an idea called "inflation" in an attempt to address the flatness and monopole problems (as well as other problems not addressed in detail here, such as the horizon problem). Inflation proposes that the universe temporarily went through a period of accelerated expansion. Amazingly, there is no real supporting evidence for inflation; it appears to be nothing more than an unsubstantiated conjecture—much like the big bang itself. Moreover, the inflation idea has difficulties of its own, such as what would start it and how it would stop smoothly. In addition, other problems with the big bang are not solved, even if inflation were true. These are examined below.

Where is the antimatter?

Consider the "baryon number problem." Recall that the big bang supposes that matter (hydrogen and helium gas) was created from energy as the universe expanded. However, experimental physics tells us that whenever matter is created from energy, such a reaction also produces *antimatter*. Antimatter has similar properties to matter, except the charges of the particles are reversed. (So whereas a proton has a positive charge, an antiproton has a *negative* charge.) Any reaction where energy is transformed into matter produces an exactly equal amount of antimatter; there are no known exceptions.

The big bang (which has no matter to begin with—only energy) should have produced exactly equal amounts of matter and antimatter, and that should be what we see today. But we do not. The visible universe is comprised almost entirely of matter—with only trace amounts of antimatter anywhere.

This devastating problem for the big bang is actually consistent with biblical creation; it is a design feature. God created the universe to be essentially matter only—and it's a good thing He did. When matter and antimatter come together, they violently destroy each other. If the universe had equal amounts of matter and antimatter (as the big bang requires), life would not be possible.

Missing Population III stars

The big bang model by itself can only account for the existence of the three lightest elements (hydrogen, helium and trace amounts of lithium). This leaves about 90 or so of the other naturally occurring elements to be explained. Since the conditions in the big bang are not right to form these heavier elements (as big bang supporters readily concede), secular astronomers believe that stars have produced the remaining elements by nuclear fusion in the core. This is thought to occur in the final stages of a massive star as it explodes (a supernova). The explosion then distributes the heavier elements into space. Second and third generation stars are thus "contaminated" with small amounts of these heavier elements.

If this story were true, then the *first* stars would have been comprised of only the three lightest elements (since these would have been the only elements in existence initially). Some such stars[3] should still be around today since their potential lifespan is calculated to exceed the (big bang) age of the universe. Such stars would be called "Population III" stars.[4] Amazingly (to those who believe in the big bang), Population III stars have not been found anywhere. All known stars have at least trace amounts of heavy elements in them. It is amazing to think that our galaxy alone is estimated to have over 100 billion stars in it. Yet not one star has been discovered that is comprised of *only* the three lightest elements.

The collapse of the big bang

With all the problems listed above, as well as many others too numerous to include, it is not surprising that quite a few secular astronomers are beginning to abandon the big bang. Although it is still the dominant model at present, increasing numbers of physicists and astronomers are realizing that the big bang simply is not a good explanation of how the universe began. In the May 22, 2004 issue of *New Scientist*, there appeared an open letter to the scientific community written primarily by *secular* scientists[5] who challenge the big bang. These scientists pointed out that the copious arbitrary assumptions and the lack of successful big bang predictions challenge the legitimacy of the model. Among other things, they state:

> The big bang today relies on a growing number of hypothetical entities, things that we have never observed—inflation, dark matter and dark energy are the most prominent examples. Without them, there would be a fatal contradiction between the observations made by astronomers and the predictions of the big bang theory. In

no other field of physics would this continual recourse to new hypothetical objects be accepted as a way of bridging the gap between theory and observation. It would, at the least, raise serious questions about the validity of the underlying theory.[6]

This statement has since been signed by hundreds of other scientists and professors at various institutions. The big bang seems to be losing considerable popularity. Secular scientists are increasingly rejecting the big bang in favor of other models. If the big bang is abandoned, what will happen to all the Christians who compromised and claimed that the Bible is compatible with the big bang? What will they say? Will they claim that the Bible actually does not teach the big bang, but instead that it teaches the latest secular model? Secular models come and go, but God's Word does not need to be changed because God got it exactly right the first time.

Conclusion

The big bang has many scientific problems. These problems are symptomatic of the underlying incorrect worldview. The big bang erroneously assumes that the universe was not supernaturally created, but that it came about by natural processes billions of years ago. However, reality does not line up with this notion. Biblical creation explains the evidence in a more straightforward way without the ubiquitous speculations prevalent in secular models. But ultimately, the best reason to reject the big bang is that it goes against what the Creator of the universe Himself has taught: "In the beginning, God created the heaven and the earth" (Genesis 1:1).

1. The sun and stars were made on Day 4 (Genesis 1:14–19). The earth was made on Day 1 (Genesis 1:1–5). Trees were made on Day 3 (Genesis 1:11–13).

2. Despite the name "heat death," the universe would actually be exceedingly cold.

3. Small (red main sequence) stars do not use up their fuel quickly. These stars theoretically have enough fuel to last significantly longer than the estimated age of the (big bang) universe.

4. If a star has a very small amount of heavy elements, it is called a "Population II" star. Pop. II stars exist primarily in the central bulge of spiral galaxies, in globular star clusters and in elliptical galaxies. If a star has a relatively large amount of heavy elements (like the sun) it is called "Population I." These stars exist primarily in the arms of spiral galaxies. The (hypothetical) Pop. III star would have no heavy elements at all.

5. The alternatives to the big bang that these scientists had suggested are equally unbiblical. These included a steady-state theory and plasma cosmology.

6. Lerner, E., et al., "An open letter to the scientific community," *New Scientist* 182(2448):20, May 22, 2004. Available online at www.cosmologystatement.org.

The Stars of Heaven Confirm Biblical Creation

by Jason Lisle

Most universities teach that stars formed from collapsing clouds of hydrogen gas billions of years ago and that stars continue to form today. Most people are unaware that there are serious scientific problems with such notions. A careful examination of the evidence confirms that stars are not billions of years old. The properties of stars do not suggest an evolutionary origin; rather, they reveal the power and majesty of the Lord.

When we peer into a clear autumn night sky and see thousands of nuclear furnaces shining like tiny gems suspended in the expanse of heaven, we should be reminded that the universe is thousands—not billions—of years old, and was supernaturally created by Almighty God. As we examine the properties of stars, we will find that they are what we would expect from Scripture.

Stars differ in glory

Let's begin by exploring some of the properties of stars and how these confirm biblical teachings. *1 Corinthians 15:41* states that one star differs from another star in glory. Although there are over one hundred billion stars in our galaxy, each one is unique. Even to the unaided eye, stars differ one from another in color and in brightness.

Stars differ in color

Stars range in color from red to blue. The color of a star indicates the surface temperature, spanning from 3,000 to 40,000 Kelvins (7,200 to 36,000°F). The coolest stars are red. Hotter stars are orange, then yellow, white, and finally blue. Our sun is intermediate, with a surface temperature of around 6,000 Kelvins (11,000°F).

Stars differ in brightness

Stars range in brightness as well as color. The intrinsic brightness (how bright a star really is) is determined by both the temperature and size of the star. Hot blue stars shine brighter than cool red stars of equal size. Big stars ("supergiants") shine brighter than little stars ("dwarfs") of equal temperature. This is because large stars have more surface area. The range of the intrinsic brightness of stars is incredible. The faint red dwarf star Proxima Centauri shines 20,000 times fainter than the sun, whereas the blue supergiant Deneb shines 200,000 times brighter![1]

The apparent brightness of a star (how bright it looks in our night sky) depends on both its distance and its intrinsic brightness. So, the brightest stars we can see are either nearby or very bright intrinsically. Since over 99% of the stars we see in the night sky are intrinsically brighter than the sun, you might think that the sun is fainter than most other stars.[2] But this isn't so. The vast majority of stars in the universe are actually fainter than the sun; in fact 47 of the 50 nearest stars are fainter.[3] In our night sky, we see more of the rare, extremely bright stars simply because they are much easier to see than the faint ones.

Stars were of supernatural origin

The properties of stars also confirm the biblical teaching that these objects were supernaturally created. Stars are made almost entirely of hydrogen and helium gas; these are the two lightest and most common elements. The combined mass from all this gas gives the star a gravitational field much stronger than earth's. This gravity prevents the gas from dispersing into space.

Secular astronomers believe that stars form spontaneously from the collapse of a nebula. A nebula is an enormous "cloud" of extremely low-density hydrogen and helium gas. If there were a way to compress such gas, then its own gravity would keep it together—a star would form. However, such compression would be very difficult to accomplish because gas has a tendency to expand, not contract. In fact, if a gas cloud were to begin to be compressed, it would drastically increase its pressure, magnetic field, and rotation speed. All of these factors would strongly resist any further compression. The compression of a nebula would be stopped long before any star could form.

Therefore, many creation scientists are convinced that stars cannot form spontaneously under normal circumstances. And despite claims to the contrary, we've never seen a star forming.[4] Star formation seems to be nothing more than a secular attempt to explain the universe without invoking God. However, the Bible tells us that the stars did not form by themselves; God supernaturally created them on the fourth day of creation (*Genesis 1:14-19*).

Stars are young

Blue stars could last only a few million years at most; however, they are found in spiral galaxies thought to be billions of years old.

Stars also confirm that creation was relatively recent, not billions of years ago. Of all the stars, blue stars present the biggest challenge for those who believe in an old universe.[5] They are the most luminous and massive type of star. Although they have more fuel available, they expend it much more quickly than their yellow or red counterparts. For this reason, blue stars cannot shine very long (by secular time scales).

Astronomers estimate that hot blue stars could last a few million years at most. Yet blue stars are found throughout the arms of virtually all spiral galaxies, such as ours, which secular astronomers postulate to be billions of years old. The commonness of blue stars verifies that they were supernaturally created in the recent past. These hot, luminous stars confirm that the universe is young—much younger than the 13.7 billion years assumed by the secular models.

The "missing" Population III stars

The composition of stars also goes against the predictions of secular (evolutionary) origins scenarios. Though the main components of a star are hydrogen and helium, there are also trace amounts of heavier elements—called metals. (In astronomy, any element heavier than helium is called a "metal.") Stars like the sun consist of only about 2% metals (the rest being hydrogen and helium); these stars are called "Population I" stars and are found primarily in the disk of spiral galaxies. Some stars have even fewer metals, perhaps only one one-hundredth the amount found in the sun. These are called Population II stars; they can be found in globular clusters and in elliptical galaxies.

According to the secular model, there should be a third class of stars—Population III, which have essentially no metals at all, other than trace amounts of lithium. The reason is that the big bang is supposed to have produced only hydrogen and helium (and trace amounts of lithium); the heavier elements, like carbon and oxygen, were supposedly produced in the central core of the first stars and dispersed into space when some of those stars exploded. Therefore, the first stars should have no heavy elements at all at their surface.[6] Yet no Population III stars have been discovered. It's a perplexing problem for those who hold to the big bang. But it's totally consistent with biblical creation.

Conclusion

The properties of stars confirm that biblical history is true. Stars differ in glory, just as the Bible teaches. Secular models of star formation are riddled with theoretical difficulties, and we have yet to see a star form spontaneously. Blue stars cannot last billions of years, yet they are common in spiral galaxies, confirming that these galaxies are young. Stars are a heavenly reminder that the universe was supernaturally created, just as the Bible declares!

---

1. This estimate depends on the exact distance to the star, which is uncertain.

2. Based on a random sampling of stars under 6th magnitude from the Hipparcos Catalogue.

3. The three exceptions are Alpha Centauri (A), Sirius (A), and Procyon (A).

4. Sometimes astronomers refer to "star-forming regions" very matter-of-factly. The layman might assume that astronomers are actually seeing stars form in such regions, but this is not so. Such regions contain hot blue stars, which astronomers assume have formed from a collapsing cloud in the recent past.

5. Specifically, this refers to "main sequence" stars. The main sequence is a concept in which both a star's surface temperature and luminosity are determined entirely by its mass. Roughly 90% of stars lie on the main sequence. Other stars lie "above" (they have higher luminosity than) main sequence stars by varying degrees.

6. Current techniques (such as spectroscopy) can only determine the surface composition of a star. The surface composition of Population III stars should be metal-free since models indicate that the surface does not mix with the core.

Can We See Stars Forming?

by Wayne R. Spencer

A recent article on the Internet was entitled "Infant Stars Caught in Act of Feeding."[1] New techniques are allowing astronomers to study disks of dust and gas around stars at very high levels of detail. The European Southern Observatory's Very Large Telescope Interferometer (or VLTI) in Chile is able to measure at an angle so small, it would be like looking at the period of a sentence at a distance of 50 kilometers (31 miles). An interferometer combines the data from two or more telescopes that are separated from each other in such a way that the multiple telescopes act like one much larger telescope. A recent study looked at six stars known as Herbig Ae/Be objects, believed to be young stars still growing in size from their formation. This study was directed at finding what is happening to the dust and gas surrounding these stars.

New stars

Astronomers frequently report observations like this of "new stars" or "young stars," which assume that these stars formed within the last few *million* years. Astronomers who believe the big bang and today's other naturalistic origins theories would say stars can form in the present from clouds of dust and gas in space. Realize that no one saw these stars form. Instead, the properties of these stars, along with their location near gas and dust clouds where astronomers think that stars form, is the basis for the belief that they are recently formed stars.

Young-universe creationist physicists and astronomers tend to be skeptical of reports claiming certain stars have recently formed. These claims often make many assumptions including that 1) the age of the star is known based on today's accepted ideas of millions of years of stellar evolution and 2) that the dust disk surrounding the star had a role in the star's formation. Evolutionary scientists would often assume the dust disk formed at about the same time as the star, though astronomers were not present to observe such events in the past.

Some creation scientists might argue that stars could not form after the Creation Week. However, others would say that stars could form after the Creation Week, but would argue that the naturalistic origins theories accepted today are not adequate explanations of the process. It is true that stars and other objects we have not seen before become visible to us all the time. There are a number of scientific reasons why scientists may see a star today that could not have been seen just days or weeks earlier in the same region of the sky. In the case of these Herbig Ae/Be stars, they simply were not observed before.

Stars and disks

The recent observations of the six Herbig Ae/Be stars showed that for two cases gas was falling into the star, and, for the other four, gas was moving outward away from the star or from a disk around the star. Stars go through a variety of stages as they age. In some of these stages there are particularly strong stellar winds made up of charged particles that flow outward from the star, driving gas away from the star. However some stars are "quieter" so that gas is more likely to be pulled into the star by gravity. Either of these processes is possible in a creation view, so these observations are not surprising.

From a creation viewpoint, the interesting questions raised by these observations are about the age of the disks and which came first, the star or the disk. What was created in the Creation Week? Was it the star, the disk, or were both created by God at the same time? Was the star formed out of the disk at creation, though perhaps in a supernatural manner? Young-universe creationist scientists research these questions and have various opinions. It is important to note that just because gas is observed falling into the star, this does not necessarily mean that the disk had anything to do with the formation of the star.

There are always other possibilities that scientists with evolutionary assumptions do not consider. Disks (and clouds) of gas and dust could have been created when the stars were created, just several thousand years ago. The dust disks dissipate over time, and today, astronomers studying these disks find that the disks do not always fit their models. Recent research on dust disks has turned up examples of stars that according to accepted ideas of stellar evolution are old, yet they are observed to have extensive dust disks.[2] Astronomers have generally believed that older stars could not still have dust disks. This calls into question the old-age assumptions regarding these disks and the stars found with them. George Rieke from the University of Arizona has recently commented on this problem, "We thought young stars, about 1 million years old, would have larger, brighter discs, and older stars from 10 to 100 million years old would have fainter ones . . . But we found some young stars missing discs and some old stars with massive discs."[3]

The clouds in space that surround many stars are often as large as or larger than our entire solar system. This may suggest that the cloud has been there since creation. However, some stars are found with smaller disks of dust and gas that could have originated in a collision of planets (extrasolar planets) orbiting the star.[4] Extrasolar planets outside our own solar system are sometimes in elliptical orbits that could make planet collisions more likely than would be the case in our own solar system. There are over 200 cases of what are believed to be planets orbiting other stars.[6] The existence of planets orbiting other stars does not conflict with a creation viewpoint, though Christians have reason to be skeptical about naturalistic planet origins theories.[7]

If some disks formed from collisions since creation, these disks would be very young in age and limited in size. On the other hand, if the disks were created in the Creation Week, they would still be only several thousand years old. An age of thousands of years means that the amount of change in the disk since the beginning would be limited. This seems to agree with this report about the six Herbig Ae/Be stars, which said that some of the stars had dust present closer to the star than was expected considering the temperature.[8] It is not surprising to find evidence of gas near the star, but these observations suggest there are microscopic dust grains close to the star. Evolutionary scientists would expect that in millions of years, dust very near the star would be driven away or would be vaporized.

How young?

So, a question raised is why have the dust particles close to the star not evaporated when it is more than hot enough to vaporize them. This suggests the disks are very young indeed. To evolutionary scientists, the dust grains near the star would be perhaps hundreds of thousands to millions of years old. Over those kinds of time scales the dust could not still be so close to the star unless something keeps it from being too hot, e.g., gas shielding the dust from the star's light. This is an example of how scientists assume processes they have not observed are at work in order to explain how the observed dust could still be present. Instead, why not consider the star and the disks to be only several thousand years old, then many of the difficulties of explaining the dust disks disappear.

1. Andrea Thompson, "Infant Stars Caught in Act of Feeding," Fox News, www.foxnews.com/story/0,2933,438225,00.html.

2. "Amazing Old Stars Give Birth Again," Space.com, www.space.com/scienceastronomy/080121-mm-old-stars.html.

3. "Planets form like 'dust bunnies'," CNN.com, www.cnn.com/2004/TECH/space/10/19/planet.formation/index.html.

4. "Two Planets Suffer Violent Collision," ScienceDaily.com, www.sciencedaily.com/releases/2008/09/080923164646.htm; B. Zuckerman, Francis C. Fekel, Michael H. Williamson, Gregory W. Henry, M. P. Muno, "Planetary systems around close binary stars: the case of the very dusty, Sun-like, spectroscopic binary BD+20 307," *Astrophysical Journal* (accepted for publication, December 10, 2008), online at arxiv.org/abs/0808.1765.

5. See exoplanets.org.

6. W. Spencer, "The Existence and Origin of Extrasolar Planets," *TJ* 15 no. 1 (2001):17–25, online at www.answersingenesis.org/tj/v15/i1/extrasolar.asp.

7. S. Kraus et. al., "The Origin of Hydrogen Line Emission for Five Herbig Ae/Be Stars Spatially Resolved by VLTI/AMBER Spectro-interferometry," *Astronomy and Astrophysics* 489 (2008):1157–1173, online at arxiv.org/abs/0807.1119.

Wayne Spencer obtained his master's degree in physics from Wichita State University in Kansas. Active in creationist circles, he has taught science and math, and now works in computer technical support.

The giant elliptical galaxy M87 is located 50 million light-years away in the constellation Virgo. The object at the center of M87 fits the description of a black hole. A black hole is believed to be the "engine" that emits a brilliant jet of high-speed electrons (diagonal line across image). Photo courtesy of NASA.

Black Holes: The Evidence of Things Not Seen

by Jason Lisle

Black holes are real phenomena in our universe. These massive objects produce such a strong gravitational pull that not even light can escape.

In 1783, British scientist John Michell postulated the idea of a "dark star"—a star with gravity so strong that even light cannot escape.[1] Any light emitted from the surface of a dark star would be pulled back to the surface by gravity, so such a star would be invisible. But is it possible to have an object so massive that light cannot escape?

Bending space and time

Before Einstein, physicists thought of gravity as a force that pulled things through space. Einstein supposed that gravity is not a force at all, but rather a "bending" of space and time.

But what does it mean to "bend" space and time? In essence, this means that gravity imparts a sort of "velocity" to empty space, and matter just "goes along for the ride."

We can illustrate this with an analogy: sailboats on a lake. The surface of the water represents "empty" space. The boats represent matter. The wind represents an external force on those boats, which drives them through the water.

What makes matter move?

1. External forces move matter through space. Just as wind moves a sailboat through the water, gravity was once thought to move matter through space.

2. In reality, gravity moves space itself, pulling matter with it. Just as a sailboat moves along a flowing river even if there are no external forces, space itself moves matter.

Before Einstein, gravity was thought to be like the wind—an external force acting on matter. But Einstein suggested that gravity is an effect, not on matter but on space itself. In our analogy, this means the water itself is flowing, as on a river, and the boats just "go along for the ride."[2] They would move even if there were no wind, because the water itself carries them along.

In our analogy, photons (particles of light) can be represented by fast motorboats that have their throttle stuck open at a certain speed (see illustration below). Like light in empty space, these motorboats always travel at the same speed. But the path of those motorboats is affected if the water is moving. Similarly, gravity bends

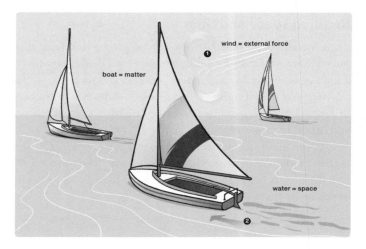

the path of light because light travels through space, and space is "moved" by gravity. We don't notice the effect of gravity bending light here on earth because earth's gravity is very weak compared to the speed of light. But the bending of light by gravity has been detected in space.

How a black hole works

This effect is merely one of several verifications of Einstein's physics; so we can have some confidence that gravity really does bend space and time as Einstein claimed. Since space itself is pulled by gravity, modern physics indicates that it is indeed possible to have a gravitational field so strong (and thus, space would be moving so fast) that light itself cannot escape. And since nothing can travel through space faster than light, nothing would be able to escape from such a powerful gravitational field. This is a "black hole"—a term coined by physicist John Wheeler in 1967.[3] Although they may seem counterintuitive, black holes are a real phenomenon.

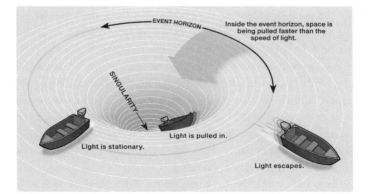

Gravity is so strong near a black hole that it pulls space inward faster than light can travel away. There is a point at which light "stops" because it is traveling outward at the same speed space is pulled inward (called the event horizon).

Since space itself is pulled by gravity, modern physics indicates that it is indeed possible to have a gravitational field so strong that light cannot escape. This is a black hole.

Black holes or dark stars?

Black holes are similar in many respects to the "dark stars" predicted by Michell, but there are some differences because our understanding of physics has improved since Michell's time. As one example, unlike Michell's conception, the actual mass of a black hole has essentially no size at all. This is because the gravity is so strong that all the mass of the "star" becomes crushed into a point called a singularity. So all the "substance" of a black hole is in the singularity.

To illustrate the physics of a black hole, let's return to our lake analogy. Imagine we pull out a giant cork in the middle of the lake and the water begins to drain. Water near the edge of the lake would be essentially unaffected. But water near the center would rapidly move toward the drain. The drain represents a massive object—the singularity.

At some small distance away from the drain, the water would be moving at the same speed as the motorboats (which represent particles of light). In other words, at this radius the water (symbolizing "space") is moving at the speed of light, which we denote by the symbol c. In a black hole, this distance is called the "Schwarzschild radius"—it's the place where space is falling into the black hole at the speed of light (c). Imagine a motorboat trying to escape by aiming away from the drain. It would be stationary because it moves at the same speed away from the water that the water is flowing toward the drain. Likewise, light that is aimed away from a black hole would be stationary at the Schwarzschild radius. It would be like salmon trying to swim upstream, but not making any headway. Objects much farther away than the Schwarzschild radius do not get pulled in; they could orbit the black hole just as planets orbit the sun. The effects of gravity pulling on space diminish with distance from the singularity just as water being pulled toward the drain is minimal far from the drain.[4]

The event horizon

The region of space corresponding to the Schwarzschild radius is called the "event horizon." It's a horizon because you can't see past it. You would never see any events that happen inside of it, since their light would never reach you.

When astronomers talk about the "size" of a black hole, they are referring to the event horizon. (Recall that the actual mass of the black hole—the singularity—has essentially no size at all!) The size of the event horizon depends on the mass of the singularity.[5]

The event horizon is the "point of no return" for a black hole. Inside the event horizon, space is being pulled toward the singularity faster than the speed of light.

(Yes, physics allows this. Although neither matter nor energy can move through space faster than light, there is no known restriction on how fast space itself can move.) Since nothing can move through space faster than light, anything inside the event horizon will be pulled toward the singularity and crushed into it—there is no escape! Even light will be pulled backwards into the singularity.

Another strange consequence of being in such a strong gravitational field is that light can actually orbit a black hole at a distance of 1.5 times the Schwarzschild radius. At this distance, light (if aimed in just the right direction) will be influenced so strongly by the black hole's gravity that it will circle around the black hole indefinitely.

Finding black holes

But if black holes are invisible, how could we ever find one? Michell suggested looking for dark stars in binary star systems. A binary star consists of two stars orbiting each other. Michell reasoned that in some binary star systems, one of the two stars would be a dark star.

Therefore, we should expect to see some visible stars orbiting around an invisible companion. And we do! One example is Cygnus X-1; here a blue supergiant star orbits around an unseen companion. The estimated mass of the invisible object indicates that it is indeed a black hole.

Many similar cases have been found. But there are other ways to detect black holes as well. For instance, material falling into the black hole can heat up and give off X-rays and other forms of radiation before it reaches the event horizon.

Some black holes have a mass comparable to a star. These stellar mass black holes may be the crushed cores of exploded stars. Other black holes are much more massive. These are commonly found in the center of galaxies. Even our own galaxy is suspected to have a super-massive black hole at its center. These galactic black holes may act as gravitational anchors for some stars in the galactic bulge.

Black holes provide an observable confirmation of Einstein's theory of general relativity. Such physics is the basis for several young-universe cosmologies, which allow light from the most distant galaxies to reach earth in thousands of years or less. Scientific discoveries, such as black holes, are not only interesting, but they give us a small glimpse into the thoughts of an infinite God (Psalm 19:1).

What is dark matter?

Astronomers have discovered that galaxies rotate faster than they would if they were comprised of only observable objects, such as stars, gas, and dust. In other words, the visible mass in most galaxies does not provide enough gravitational attraction to account for the motions we observe. This suggests that galaxies contain an invisible source of mass, called dark matter. Dark matter is any nonvisible substance that is detected only by its gravitational influence on other (visible) objects. Most astrophysicists currently believe that there is much more dark matter in the universe than visible matter.

Some physicists believe that dark matter is composed of ordinary matter, but that such matter is so cold that it does not emit enough radiation for us to detect. For example, planets or other large objects that do not radiate energy or reflect light from nearby stars would be classified as dark matter. Black holes are one example in this category. However, it is more commonly believed that most dark matter is composed of exotic, as-yet-undiscovered particles that permeate the universe. This is called nonbaryonic dark matter because, unlike ordinary atoms, it would not be made of protons and neutrons (which are baryons).

Some scientists have suggested alternatives to dark matter. For example, it may be that the laws of physics are slightly different than currently understood, as suggested by the MOND[1] and Carmelian[2] models. If either of these models is correct, then there may be very little dark matter in the universe. Such a result would be devastating to big bang models since these require copious quantities of dark matter. However, most creation models of cosmology would work either way.

1. MOND stands for "modified Newtonian dynamics." Technically, it proposes that the acceleration of gravity deviates from the usual inverse square law for very low accelerations.

2. Carmelian physics is a five-dimensional variation on general relativity, which proposes that expansion is an intrinsic property of the universe.

1.   The concept was also proposed independently by Pierre-Simon LaPlace in 1799.

2.   This analogy is mathematically rigorous when we assign the speed of the water (space) to be the escape velocity. This is called the "river model of black holes" and was developed by Andrew Hamilton and Jason Lisle; see A. J. S. Hamilton and J. Lisle, "The River Model of Black Holes" in *General Relativity and Quantum Cosmology*, online at arxiv.org/abs/gr-qc/0411060v2.

3.   K. Thorne, *Black Holes and Time Warps: Einstein's Outrageous Legacy* (New York: W. W. Norton & Company, 1994), p. 256.

4.   If the sun could be compressed into a black hole (of equal mass), the planets would not be pulled in; they would continue in their present orbits because they are far away from the Schwarzschild radius.

5.   The Schwarzschild radius for a mass M is given by $R_s = 2GM/c^2$ where G is the universal gravitational constant and c is the speed of light. Visit www.answersingenesis.org/articles/am/v3/n1/lens to see a black hole gravity lens.

Does Distant Starlight Prove the Universe Is Old?

by Jason Lisle

Critics of biblical creation sometimes use distant starlight as an argument against a young universe. The argument goes something like this: (1) there are galaxies that are so far away, it would take light from their stars billions of years to get from there to here; (2) we can see these galaxies, so their starlight has already arrived here; and (3) the universe must be at least billions of years old—much older than the 6,000 or so years indicated in the Bible.

Many big bang supporters consider this to be an excellent argument against the biblical timescale. But when we examine this argument carefully, we will see that it does not work. The universe is very big and contains galaxies that are very far away, but that does not mean that the universe must be billions of years old.

The distant starlight question has caused some people to question cosmic distances. "Do we really know that galaxies are so far away? Perhaps they are much closer, so the light really doesn't travel very far."[1] However, the techniques that astronomers use to measure cosmic distances are generally logical and scientifically sound. They do not rely on evolutionary assumptions about the past. Moreover, they are a part of *observational* science (as opposed to historical/origins science); they are testable and repeatable in the present. You could repeat the experiment to determine the distance to a star or galaxy, and you would get approximately the same answer. So we have good reason to believe that space really is very big. In fact, the amazing size of the universe brings glory to God (Psalm 19:1).

Some Christians have proposed that God created the beams of light from distant stars already on their way to the earth. After all, Adam didn't need any time to grow from a baby because he was made as an adult. Likewise, it is argued that the universe was made mature, and so perhaps the light was created in-transit. Of course, the universe was indeed made to function right from the first week, and many aspects of it were indeed created "mature." The only problem with assuming that the light was created in-transit is that we see things happen in space. For example, we see stars change brightness and move. Sometimes we see stars explode. We see these things because their light has reached us.

But if God created the light beams already on their way, then that means none of the events we see in space (beyond a distance of 6,000 light-years) actually happened. It would mean that those exploding stars never exploded or existed; God merely painted pictures of these fictional events. It seems uncharacteristic of God to make illusions like this. God made our eyes to accurately probe the real universe; so we can trust that the events that we see in space really happened. For this reason, most creation scientists believe that light created in-transit is not the best way to respond to the distant starlight argument. Let me suggest that the answer to distant starlight lies in some of the unstated assumptions that secular astronomers make.

The assumptions of light travel-time arguments

Any attempt to scientifically estimate the age of something will necessarily involve a number of *assumptions*. These can be assumptions about the starting conditions, constancy of rates, contamination of the system, and many others. If even one of these assumptions is wrong, so is the age estimate. Sometimes an incorrect worldview is to blame when people make faulty assumptions. The distant starlight argument involves several assumptions that are questionable—any one of which makes the argument unsound. Let's examine a few of these assumptions.

The constancy of the speed of light

It is usually assumed that the speed of light is constant with time.[2] At today's rate, it takes light (in a vacuum) about one year to cover a distance of 6 trillion miles. But has this always been so? If we incorrectly assume that the rate has always been today's rate, we would end up estimating an age that is much older than the true age. But some people have proposed that light was much quicker in the past. If so, light could traverse the universe in only a fraction of the time it would take today. Some creation scientists believe that this is the answer to the problem of distant starlight in a young universe.

However, the speed of light is not an "arbitrary" parameter. In other words, changing the speed of light would cause other things to change as well, such as the ratio of energy to mass in any system.[3] Some people have argued that the speed of light can never have been much different than it is today because it is so connected to other constants of nature. In other words, life may not be possible if the speed of light were any different.

This is a legitimate concern. The way in which the universal constants are connected is only partially understood. So, the impact of a changing speed of light on the universe and life on earth is not fully known. Some creation scientists are actively researching questions relating to the speed of light. Other creation scientists feel that the assumption of the constancy of the speed of light is probably reasonable and that the solution to distant starlight lies elsewhere.

The assumption of rigidity of time

Many people assume that time flows at the same rate in all conditions. At first, this seems like a very reasonable assumption. But, in fact, this assumption is false. And there are a few different ways in which the nonrigid nature of time could allow distant starlight to reach earth within the biblical timescale.

Albert Einstein discovered that the rate at which time passes is affected by motion and by gravity. For example, when an object moves very fast, close to the speed of light, its time is slowed down. This is called "time-dilation." So, if we were able to accelerate a clock to nearly the speed of light, that clock would tick very slowly. If we could somehow reach the speed of light, the clock would stop completely. This isn't a problem with the clock; the effect would happen regardless of the clock's particular construction because it is time itself that is slowed. Likewise, gravity slows the passage of time. A clock at sea-level would tick slower than one on a mountain, since the clock at sea-level is closer to the source of gravity.

It seems hard to believe that velocity or gravity would affect the passage of time since our everyday experience cannot detect this. After all, when we are traveling in a vehicle, time appears to flow at the same rate as when we are standing still. But that's because we move so slowly compared to the speed of light, and the earth's gravity is so weak that the effects of time-dilation are correspondingly tiny. However, the effects of time-dilation have been measured with atomic clocks.

Since time can flow at different rates from different points of view, events that would take a long time as measured by one person will take very little time as measured by another person. This also applies to distant starlight. Light that would take billions of years to reach earth (as measured by clocks in deep space) could reach earth in only thousands of years as measured by clocks on earth. This would happen naturally if the earth is in a *gravitational well*, which we will discuss below.

Many secular astronomers assume that the universe is infinitely big and has an infinite number of galaxies. This has never been proven, nor is there evidence that would lead us naturally to that conclusion. So, it is a leap of "blind" faith on their part. However, if we make a different assumption instead, it leads to a very different conclusion. Suppose that our solar system is located near the center of a finite distribution of galaxies. Although this cannot be proven for certain at present, it is fully consistent with the evidence; so it is a reasonable possibility.

In that case, the earth would be in a gravitational well. This term means that it would require energy to pull something away from our position into deeper space. In this gravitational well, we would not "feel" any extra gravity, nonetheless time would flow more slowly on earth (or anywhere in our solar system) than in other places of the universe. This effect is thought to be very small today; however, it may have been much stronger in the past. (If the universe is expanding as most astronomers believe, then physics demands that such effects would have been stronger when the universe was smaller). This being the case, clocks on earth would have ticked much more slowly than clocks in deep space. Thus, light from the most distant galaxies would arrive on earth in only a few thousand years as measured by clocks on earth. This idea is certainly intriguing. And although there are still a number of mathematical details that need to be worked out, the premise certainly is reasonable. Some creation scientists are actively researching this idea.

Assumptions of synchronization

Another way in which the relativity of time is important concerns the topic of synchronization: how clocks are set so that they read the same time at the same time.[4] Relativity has shown that synchronization is not absolute. In other words, if one person measures two clocks to be synchronized, another person (moving at a different speed) would *not* necessarily measure those two clocks to be synchronized. As with time-dilation, this effect is counterintuitive because it is too small to measure in most of our everyday experience. Since there is no method by which two clocks (separated by a distance) can be synchronized in an absolute sense, such that all observers would agree regardless of motion, it follows that there is some flexibility in how we choose what constitutes synchronized clocks. The following analogy may be helpful.

Imagine that a plane leaves a certain city at 4:00 p.m. for a two-hour flight. However, when the plane lands, the time is still 4:00. Since the plane arrived at the same time it left, we might call this an instantaneous trip. How is this possible? The answer has to do with time zones. If the plane left Kentucky at 4:00 p.m. local time, it would arrive in Colorado at 4:00 p.m. local time. Of course, an observer on the plane would experience two hours of travel. So, the trip takes two hours as measured by *universal time*. However, as long as the plane is traveling west (and providing it travels fast enough), it will always naturally arrive at the same time it left as measured in *local time*.

There is a cosmic equivalent to local and universal time. Light traveling toward earth is like the plane traveling west; it always remains at the same cosmic local time. Although most astronomers today primarily use cosmic universal time (in which it takes light 100 years to travel 100 light-years), historically cosmic local time has been the standard. And so it may be that the Bible also uses cosmic local time when reporting events.

Since God created the stars on Day 4, their light would leave the star on Day 4 and reach earth on Day 4 *cosmic local time*. Light from all galaxies would reach earth on Day 4 if we measure it according to cosmic local time. Someone might object that the light itself would experience billions of years (as the passenger on the plane experiences the two hour trip). However, according to Einstein's relativity, light does not experience the passage of time, so the trip would be instantaneous. Now, this idea may or may not be the reason that distant starlight is able to reach earth within the biblical timescale, but so far no one has been able to prove that the Bible does *not* use cosmic local time. So, it is an intriguing possibility.[5]

The assumption of naturalism

One of the most overlooked assumptions in most arguments against the Bible is the assumption of *naturalism*. Naturalism is the belief that nature is "all that there is." Proponents of naturalism *assume* that all phenomena can be explained in terms of natural laws. This is not only a blind assumption, but it is also clearly antibiblical. The Bible makes it clear that God is not bound by natural laws (they are, after all, *His* laws). Of course God can use laws of nature to accomplish His will; and He usually does so. In fact, natural laws could be considered a description of the way in which God normally upholds the universe. But God is supernatural and is capable of acting outside natural law.

This would certainly have been the case during Creation Week. God created the universe supernaturally. He created it from nothing, not from previous material (Hebrews 11:3). Today, we do not see God speaking into existence new stars or new kinds of creatures. This is because God ended His work of creation by the seventh day. Today, God sustains the universe in a different way than how He created it. However, the naturalist erroneously assumes that the universe was created by the same processes by which it operates today. Of course it would be absurd to apply this assumption to most other things. A flashlight, for example, operates by converting electricity into light, but the flashlight was not created by this process.

Since the stars were created during Creation Week and since God made them to give light upon the earth, the way in which distant starlight arrived on earth may have been supernatural. We cannot assume that past acts of God are necessarily understandable in terms of a current scientific mechanism, because science can only probe the way in which God sustains the universe today. It is irrational to argue that a supernatural act cannot be true on the basis that it cannot be explained by natural processes observed today.

It is perfectly acceptable for us to ask, "Did God use natural processes to get the starlight to earth in the biblical timescale? And if so, what is the mechanism?" But if no natural mechanism is apparent, this cannot be used as evidence against *supernatural* creation. So, the unbeliever is engaged in a subtle form of circular reasoning when he uses the assumption of naturalism to argue that distant starlight disproves the biblical timescale.

Light travel-time: a self-refuting argument

Many big bang supporters use the above assumptions to argue that the biblical timescale cannot be correct because of the light travel-time issue. But such an argument is self-refuting. It is fatally flawed because the big bang has a light travel-time problem of its own. In the big bang model, light is required to travel a distance much greater than should be possible within the big bang's own timeframe of about 14 billion years. This serious difficulty for the big bang is called the "horizon problem." [6] The following are the details.

In the big bang model, the universe begins in an infinitely small state called a singularity, which then rapidly expands. According to the big bang model, when the universe is still very small, it would develop different temperatures in different locations (Figure 1). Let's suppose that point A is hot and point B is cold. Today, the universe has expanded (Figure 2), and points A and B are now widely separated.

However, the universe has an extremely uniform temperature at great distance— beyond the farthest known galaxies. In other words, points A and B have almost exactly the same temperature

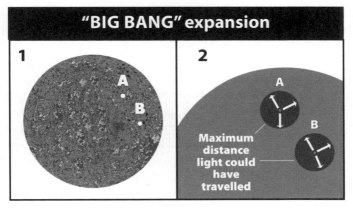

"BIG BANG" expansion

1

2

A

B

Maximum distance light could have travelled

today. We know this because we see electromagnetic radiation coming from all directions in space in the form of microwaves. This is called the "cosmic microwave background" (CMB). The frequencies of radiation have a characteristic temperature of 2.7 K (-455°F) and are *extremely* uniform in all directions. The temperature deviates by only one part in 10^5.

The problem is this: How did points A and B come to be the same temperature? They can do this only by exchanging energy. This happens in many systems: consider an ice cube placed in hot coffee. The ice heats up and the coffee cools down by exchanging energy. Likewise, point A can give energy to point B in the form of electromagnetic radiation (light), which is the fastest way to transfer energy since nothing can travel faster than light. However, using the big bang supporters' own assumptions, including uniformitarianism and naturalism, there has not been enough time in 14 billion years to get light from A to B; they are too far apart. This is a light travel-time problem—and a very serious one. After all, A and B have almost exactly the same temperature today, and so must have exchanged light multiple times.

Big bang supporters have proposed a number of conjectures which attempt to solve the big bang's light travel-time problem. One of the most popular is called "inflation." In "inflationary" models, the universe has two expansion rates: a normal rate and a fast inflation rate. The universe begins with the normal rate, which is actually quite rapid, but is slow by comparison to the next phase. Then it briefly enters the inflation phase, where the universe expands much more rapidly. At a later time, the universe goes back to the normal rate. This all happens early on, long before stars and galaxies form.

The inflation model allows points A and B to exchange energy (during the first normal expansion) and to then be pushed apart during the inflation phase to the enormous distances at which they are located today. But the inflation model amounts to nothing more than storytelling with no supporting evidence at all. It is merely speculation designed to align the big bang to conflicting observations. Moreover, inflation adds an additional set of problems and difficulties to the big bang model, such as the cause of such inflation and a graceful way to turn it off. An increasing number of secular astrophysicists are rejecting inflation for these reasons and others. Clearly, the horizon problem remains a serious light travel-time problem for the big bang.

The critic may suggest that the big bang is a better explanation of origins than the Bible since biblical creation has a light travel-time problem—distant starlight. But such an argument is not rational since the big bang has a light travel-time problem of its own. If both models have the same problem *in essence*[7], then that problem cannot be used to support one model over the other. Therefore, distant starlight cannot be used to dismiss the Bible in favor of the big bang.

Conclusions

So, we've seen that the critics of creation must use a number of assumptions in order to use distant starlight as an argument against a young universe. And many of these assumptions are questionable. Do we know that light has always propagated at today's speed? Perhaps this is reasonable, but can we be absolutely certain, particularly during Creation Week when God was acting in a supernatural way? Can we be certain that the Bible is using "cosmic universal time," rather than the more common "cosmic local time" in which light reaches earth instantly?

We know that the rate at which time flows is not rigid. And although secular astronomers are well aware that time is relative, they *assume* that this effect is (and has always been) negligible, but can we be certain that this is so? And since stars were made during Creation Week when God was *supernaturally* creating, how do we know for certain that distant starlight has arrived on earth by entirely *natural* means? Furthermore, when big bang supporters use distant starlight to argue against biblical creation, they are using a self-refuting argument since the big bang has a light travel-time problem of its own. When we consider all of the above, we see that distant starlight has never been a legitimate argument against the biblical timescale of a few thousand years.

As creation scientists research possible solutions to the distant starlight problem, we should also remember the body of evidence that is consistent with the youth of the universe. We see rotating spiral galaxies that cannot last multiple billions of years because they would be twisted-up beyond recognition. We see multitudes of hot blue stars, which even secular astronomers would agree cannot last billions of years.[8] In our own solar system we see disintegrating comets and decaying magnetic fields that cannot last billions of years; and there is evidence that other solar systems have these things as well. Of course, such arguments also involve assumptions about the past. That is why, ultimately, the only way to know about the past *for certain* is to have a reliable historic record written by an eyewitness. That is exactly what we have in the Bible.

1.   See the DVD *Astronomy: What Do We Really Know?* by Dr. Jason Lisle for a more complete treatment of these questions, available at www.AnswersBookstore.com.

2.   Many people mistakenly think that Einstein's theory of relativity demands that the speed of light has not changed in time. In reality, this is not so. Relativity only requires that two different observers would measure the same velocity for a beam of light, even if they are moving relative to each other.

3.   This follows from the equation $E=mc^2$, in which c is the speed of light and E is the energy associated with a given amount of mass (m).

4.   For a discussion on synchrony conventions see W.C. Salmon, "The philosophical significance of the one-way speed of light," *Nous* 11(3):253–292, Symposium on Space and Time, 1977.

5.   See "Distant Starlight and Genesis," *TJ* 15(1):80–85, 2001, online at www.answersingenesis.org/tj/v15/i1/starlight.asp.

6.   See www.answersingenesis.org/creation/v25/i4/lighttravel.asp.

7.   The details, of course, differ. The big bang does not have a problem with distant starlight as such. But then again, biblical creation does not have a horizon problem. (The cosmic microwave background does not need to start with different temperatures in a creationist cosmogony.) However, both problems are the same in essence: how to get light to travel a greater distance than seems possible in the time allowed.

8.   Secular astronomers believe that blue stars must have formed relatively recently. But there are considerable difficulties in star formation scenarios—problems with magnetic fields and angular momentum to name a couple.

The Star of Bethlehem: A Supernatural Sign in the Heavens?

by Jason Lisle

Matthew was one of the twelve apostles. He also wrote the first book of the New Testament. In that book, he recorded that the birth of Jesus was accompanied by an extraordinary celestial event: a star led the magi (the "wise men") to Jesus. This star "went before them, till it came and stood over where the young child was" (Matthew 2:9). What was this star? And how did it lead the magi to the Lord? There have been many speculations.

Common explanations

Explanations for the event include a supernova, a comet, a massing of planets, a triple conjunction of Jupiter and Regulus (a bright star in the constellation Leo), or the astonishing conjunction of Jupiter and Venus on June 17, 2 BC. Although each of these events is truly spectacular and may have been fitting to announce the birth of the King of Kings, none of them seems to fully satisfy the details of the straightforward reading of Matthew 2. None of the above speculations fully explain how the star "went ahead of" the magi nor how it "stood over where the child was." Indeed no known natural phenomenon would be able to stand over Bethlehem since all "natural" stars continually move due to the rotation of the earth.[1] They appear to rise in the east and set in the west, or circle around the celestial poles. However, the Bible does not say that this star was a *natural* phenomenon.

Natural law

Of course, God can use natural law to accomplish His will. In fact, a biblical definition of natural law is the way that God normally upholds the universe and accomplishes His will, but God is not bound by the laws He created; He may (and does on occasion) temporarily suspend those laws when He has an important reason to do so.

The Virgin Birth itself was a supernatural event; it cannot be explained within the context of known natural laws. And it should not be surprising that the birth of the Son of God would be accompanied by a supernatural sign in the heavens. The star that led the magi seems to be one of those incredible acts of God—specially designed and created for a unique purpose.[2] Let us examine what this star did according to Matthew 2.

Purpose of the star

First, the star alerted the magi to the birth of Christ, prompting them to make the long trek to Jerusalem. These magi were "from the East" according to verse 1; they are generally thought to be from Persia, which is east of Jerusalem. If so, they may have had some knowledge of the Scriptures since the prophet Daniel had also lived in that region centuries earlier. Perhaps the magi were expecting a new star to announce the birth of Christ from reading Numbers 24:17, which describes a star coming from Jacob and a King ("scepter")[3] from Israel.[4]

Ethereal or physical

Curiously, the magi seem to have been the only ones who saw the star—or at least the only ones who understood its meaning. Israel's King Herod had to ask the magi when the star had appeared (Matthew 2:7). If the magi alone saw the star, this further supports the notion that the star of Bethlehem was a supernatural manifestation from God rather than a common star, which would have been visible to all.

Clearing up misconceptions

Contrary to what is commonly believed, the magi did not arrive at the manger on the night of Christ's birth; rather, they found the young Jesus and His parents living in a house (Matthew 2:11). This could have been nearly two years after Christ's birth, since Herod—afraid that his own position as king was threatened—tried to have Jesus eliminated by killing all male children under the age of two (Matthew 2:16).

It may be that the star first appeared over Bethlehem when the magi were in the East (Persia).[5,6] From that distance, they would not have been able to distinguish the exact location but would certainly have known to head west. They went to Israel's capital city Jerusalem, a likely place to begin their search for the King of the Jews.

It seems that the star may have disappeared by the time the magi reached Jerusalem but then reappeared when they began their (much shorter) journey from Jerusalem to Bethlehem, approximately 6 miles (10 km) away. This view is supported by the fact that first, the magi had to ask King Herod where the King of the Jews was born, which means the star wasn't guiding them at that time (Matthew 2:2). And second, they rejoiced exceedingly when they saw the star (again) as they began their journey to Bethlehem (Matthew 2:10).

After the magi had met with Herod, the star went on before them to Bethlehem and stood over the location of Jesus. It seems to have led them to the very house that Jesus was in—not just the city. The magi already knew that Christ was in Bethlehem. This they had learned from Herod, who had learned it from the priests and scribes (Matthew 2:4–5). For a normal star, it would be impossible to determine which house is directly beneath it. The star over Christ may have been relatively near the surface of earth (an "atmospheric" manifestation of God's power) so that the magi could discern the precise location of the Child.

Whatever the exact mechanism, the fact that the star led the magi to Christ is evidence that the star was uniquely designed, made by God for a very special purpose. God can use extraordinary means for extraordinary purposes. Certainly the birth of our Lord was deserving of honor in the heavens. It is fitting that God used a celestial object to announce the birth of Christ since "the heavens declare the glory of God . . . ." (Psalm 19:1).

---

1. The star that moves the least is the North Star because it is almost directly in line with the earth's North Pole. However, this would not have been the case at the time of Christ's birth due to a celestial phenomenon called "precession."

2. Although this star seems to break all the rules, it is perhaps even more amazing that essentially all the other stars do not. The fact that all the stars in our night sky obey orderly logical laws of nature is consistent with biblical creation. (For more information on the laws of nature, see "God & Natural Law" online at www.answersingenesis.org/articles/am/v1/n2/God-natural-law.)

3. This verse makes use of synecdoche—the part represents the whole. In this case, the scepter represents a scepter-bearer, i.e., a king. This is clear from the synonymous parallelism (see the next note).

4. This verse is written in a poetic way; it uses synonymous parallelism (star and scepter=Israel and Jacob).

5. The position of the star when the magi first saw it is disputed. It could be that the star was in the eastward heavens when they first saw it, or it could be that the magi were "in the East" (i.e., Persia) when they saw the star. (The latter view is indicated by John Gill in his commentary.) If it was the star that was in the East, why did the magi travel west? Recall that the Bible does not say that the star guided the magi to Jerusalem (though it may have); we only know for certain that it went before them to Bethlehem. It is possible that the star initially acted only as a sign, rather than as a guide. The magi may have headed to Jerusalem only because this would have seemed a logical place to begin their search for the King of the Jews.

6. It is also possible that the star may have appeared in the western sky while the magi were in the East, giving them the direction to travel. Furthermore, the Greek words translated "in the East" can also be translated "at its rising." So it could be that the magi saw the star at its rising. All ordinary stars rise in the East (due to earth's rotation), but this was no ordinary star and may have risen in the West over Bethlehem, or Jerusalem (which from the distance of Persia would have been indistinguishable). Such a strange rising would certainly have distinguished this star as unique as it "rose out of Israel," which fits nicely with Numbers 24:17.

The Gospel Message— Written in the Stars?

by Danny Faulkner

Since early in history, humans have studied the stars and given names to the unique groupings called constellations. We do not know who originated the names of constellations or the names of the more famous stars, but there are many theories.

The gospel in the stars theory

One theory, proposed in the nineteenth century, was that the constellations represent the vestiges of a primal gospel that God gave to early man. We call this view the "gospel in the stars." According to this theory, God presented His full plan of salvation to Adam, and either Adam or his early descendents preserved that knowledge by naming the constellations and stars. With the coming of the written Word of God, the gospel message in the stars was no longer needed and faded from use. With the passage of time, ungodly men perverted the original gospel in the stars, mingling it with pagan mythology and ultimately turning it into the religion of astrology.

The English woman Frances Rolleston supposedly rediscovered this long-hidden truth and published her work 140 years ago in *Mazzaroth*. Many authors since then have uncritically accepted Rolleston's work.

Fast facts

- By modern conventions, there are actually thirteen constellations in the Zodiac; Ophiuchus is normally omitted when the Zodiac is listed.

- Ancient star charts reveal that earth's axis gradually precesses over the centuries. For this reason, there has been a "North Star" for only a few centuries.

Rolleston assumed that Hebrew is the closest language to that of Adam, which is a common belief among Christians but is not necessarily true. She also assumed that pronunciation and little else was altered at Babel. Based on these assumptions, Rolleston searched the Hebrew language for similar-sounding words in other languages (homophones) to match star and constellation names.

For instance, Rolleston reasoned that Latin was derived from Etruscan, which was derived from Assyrian, and since Assyrian was a Semitic language, it was probably derived from Hebrew. Thus, Rolleston thought that she could find meanings of Latin names from Hebrew roots. Given the highly speculative nature of this approach, her conclusions on particular meanings from Hebrew are very suspect at best.

Rolleston's method

As an example of Rolleston's methodology, consider the meaning that she found for the star Deneb, the brightest star in the constellation Cygnus. She reasoned that it was a perversion of the Hebrew *dan*, which means "judge." Because Hebrew scribes added marks for vowels much later, one could suppose that this is possible. However, why search for some other meaning when the traditional Arabic meaning works so well? The Arab word *deneb* means "tail," and it marks the tail of Cygnus. Incidentally, several other stars contain deneb as a portion of their names, and in each case they mark the tails of their respective constellations. Yet Rolleston persisted with her reinterpretation of words.

The name *Orion* appears three times in the Bible (Job 9:9, 38:31; Amos 5:8). Rolleston correctly noted that *Chesil* is the Hebrew word translated as "Orion" in all three instances and that

Hebrew tradition generally identified Orion with Nimrod. Orion is a hunter, and Nimrod was a mighty hunter before the Lord (Genesis 10:9), so this connection makes sense.

Rolleston viewed Orion as a type of Christ. On most star charts a hare lies beneath the feet of Orion, but Rolleston noted that in some ancient charts a snake lies below his feet. Presumably, this snake has bitten, or bruised, Orion's heal, but Orion is crushing the serpent's head in fulfillment of the first messianic prophecy (Genesis 3:15). She also noted that in some mythologies Orion was stung to death by a scorpion. Some of those stories have Orion stung on the foot, but others do not specify where the scorpion stung Orion.

Errors in Rolleston's interpretation

There are several problems with this interpretation. First, a scorpion is not a snake. To claim that a scorpion illustrates Genesis 3:15 is a tremendous stretch. Second, there are other stories of Orion's demise, so Rolleston was very selective in which stories she wished to use and which she wished to ignore. Then there is the matter of the identification of Christ with Nimrod, who is hardly a positive character in the Old Testament.

The theory that the plan of salvation can be seen in the stars has several problems.

Far more problematic is the Hebrew word used for Orion. Elsewhere in the Old Testament this word is translated "fool." For instance, *chesil* is the word translated "fool" eight times in Proverbs 26. Thus, by the Hebrew name for him, we can see that Orion is not an individual worthy of respect and devotion. To equate this fool with a type of Christ borders on blasphemy, and most Christians ought to find this offensive. If Rolleston had been as proficient in Hebrew as required to do word studies, then she ought to have known that the Hebrew word for Orion is the same as a "fool."

But there is a far more serious objection to the gospel in the stars: it contradicts biblical texts. The New Testament calls the gospel a "mystery" (1 Corinthians 2:7; Ephesians 6:19, 3:8–12; Colossians 4:3). In the New Testament, a mystery is something that was previously unknown but now is revealed to us. Romans 16:25–26 states that this mystery was hidden for long ages and was revealed through prophetic writings (that is, in the Old Testament, not in the stars). 1 Corinthians 2:8 further tells us that, if the princes of this world had known of this mystery, "they would not have crucified the Lord of glory." 1 Peter 1:10–12 suggests that, while the prophets "searched diligently," they failed to grasp fully the gospel before its time.

The lesson for us

Is there anything that we can salvage from all of this? Despite the damage wrought by purveyors of the gospel in the stars, the surprising answer is yes, we can. In speaking about the constellations, such as in planetarium shows, we can make parallels to spiritual truths. For instance, a discussion of Virgo the virgin can easily lead to discussion of the conception and birth of Jesus Christ. This is not so different from using parables as Jesus did—He alluded to everyday examples that His listeners could relate to. It also is similar to what Paul did in his sermon at Mars Hill (Acts 17:23–31), where Paul took the inscription at a pagan shrine and launched into a gospel message. Paul even quoted from a poem of Aratus that described many of the constellations.

The beauty of Christ's work does not require us to embellish it with half-truths or outright errors. The key is for us to share the gospel with simplicity, integrity, and fervor.

Danny Faulkner is a professor of physics and astronomy at the University of South Carolina Lancaster. He has written numerous articles in astronomical journals, and he is the author of *Universe by Design*.

The Majesty of God

by Tom Chesko

Psalm 19:1: "To the Chief Musician. A Psalm of David. The heavens declare the glory of God; and the firmament shows His handiwork."

The word "heavens" in the first verse of Psalm 19 emphatically draws our attention immediately upward to the creation of God. David, the shepherd and author of this praise, was overcome with the majesty of the God of Abraham as his eyes focused on the works of His hand. The grandeur of God, as revealed in the natural world, is evident even to the heathen. As Romans says, "Because what may be known of God is manifest in them, for God has shown it to them. For since the creation of the world His invisible attributes are clearly seen, being understood by the things that are made, even His eternal power and Godhead, so that they are without excuse" (Romans 1:19–20).

Many of us have had an experience similar to David's when we've seen the beauty of the mountains, studied the remarkable world of animals and insects, or considered the vastness of space. As a little boy, I often peered into "outer space" with admiration and perplexity. Just what existed beyond the range of my vision and when did it get there? I often asked myself. I never doubted that God was the one who created it. As Psalm 14:1 says, only "the fool hath said in his heart, there is no God."

The advanced technology of today has allowed us to see what I could not see as a child, let alone what the men of the Bible could see only with the naked eye. I have to wonder what David would exclaim if he could see some of the hundreds of thousands of remarkable space photos taken by the Hubble telescope since its launch in 1990. What would Sir Isaac Newton (1643–1727) think were he alive today?

According to many, Newton had no equals in the history of science. A sketch of his life was presented in a Christian History Institute publication in which the author described Newton in this way:

> Among the greatest scientific geniuses of all times, Isaac Newton made major contributions to mathematics, optics, physics, and astronomy. He discovered the law of gravitation, formulated the basic laws of motion, developed calculus, and analyzed the nature of white light. Behind all his science was the conviction that God made the universe with a mathematical structure and He gifted human beings' minds to understand that structure. The very orderliness and design of the universe spoke of God's awesome majesty and wisdom.[1]

A fool denies the existence of God; Newton denied that anything could come into existence apart from God. He also understood that the greatness and power of God is beyond our comprehension. He said, "I must confess to a feeling of profound humility in the presence of a universe which transcends us at almost every point. I feel like a child who while playing by the seashore has found a few bright colored shells and a few pebbles while the whole vast ocean of truth stretches out almost untouched and unruffled before my eager fingers."

Amen to that! "Great is our Lord, and of great power: his understanding is infinite" (Psalm 147:5). "He hath made the earth by his power, he hath established the world by his wisdom, and hath stretched out the heaven by his understanding" (Jeremiah 51:15).

Certainly the God who can do such things (and so much more) must be the only object of our worship and praise. I find it no surprise that Psalm 19 was addressed "to the chief musician."

Another hymn writer Isaac Watts composed, "The Heavens Declare Thy Glory," which begins, "The heavens declare thy glory, Lord, in every star thy wisdom shines." Truly the wisdom of God shines forth in all His glorious creation.

As he contemplated the heavens above, Watts was led to bow to the ground and worship the Creator, just as David boasted of God in Psalm 19. Should we not be moved to praise God when we see the glory of His creation?

Dr. Arthur Harding, in his textbook on astronomy, asked, "Who can study the science of astronomy and contemplate the star-lit heavens with a knowledge of the dimensions of the celestial bodies, their movements and their enormous distances, without bowing his head in reverence to the power that brought this universe into being and safely guides its individual members?"[2]

The apostle Paul said in 1 Corinthians 13:11, "When I was a child, I spake as a child, I understood as a child, I thought as a child: but when I became a man, I put away childish things." I became a "new man in Christ Jesus" by trusting His sacrifice on the cross for the forgiveness of my sins (2 Corinthians 5:17; 1 Corinthians 15:3).

I too have matured in my understanding of God's majesty. I now know more fully (although still in part) that He is the Sovereign Lord of the heavens and the earth who alone is worthy of my deepest devotion, my unceasing thanks, and the consecration of my life for His glory and that of Christ who brought all things into existence and redeemed my soul (1 Peter 1:18).

Colossians 1:12–16 states:

> "Giving thanks unto the Father, which hath made us meet to be partakers of the inheritance of the saints in light: Who hath delivered us from the power of darkness, and hath translated us into the kingdom of his dear Son: In whom we have redemption through his blood, even the forgiveness of sins: Who is the image of the invisible God,

the firstborn of every creature: For by him were all things created, that are in heaven, and that are in earth, visible and invisible, whether they be thrones, or dominions, or principalities, or powers: all things were created by him, and for him: And he is before all things, and by him all things consist."

Brethren, never give in to fear, worry, or doubt. God has all things under control. He will safely guide us to our eternal home. The next time you look skyward remember the all-wise and loving God who brought forth the heavenly bodies, and sustains them from day to day. Catch a greater glimpse of His glory and earthly concerns will not seem so daunting!

---

1.   Christian History Institute, Glimpses #69.

2.   Arthur M. Harding, *Astronomy* (New York: Garden City Publishing Co., 1940), p. 386.

Tom Chesko has been the pastor of Faith Community Bible Church near San Diego since 1990. This is the church where Ken Ham and family attended before moving to Kentucky to begin Answers in Genesis. Tom has remained a personal friend and confidant of the Ham family, and is also a great friend of AiG.

Are ETs & UFOs Real?

by Jason Lisle

Are there extraterrestrial life-forms out there? The question of life on other planets is a hot topic in our culture today. Science fiction movies and television shows often depict strange creatures from far-away planets. But these ideas are not limited merely to science fiction programming. Many secular scientists believe that one day we will actually discover life on other planets. There are even projects like the Search for Extra-Terrestrial Intelligence (SETI) that scan the heavens with powerful radio telescopes listening for signals from intelligent aliens. Many Christians have bought into the idea of extraterrestrial alien life. But is this idea really biblical? The Christian should constantly examine ideas in light of Scripture and take "every thought into captivity to the obedience of Christ" (2 Corinthians 10:5).

The evolution connection

The idea of extraterrestrial life stems largely from a belief in evolution. Recall that in the evolutionary view, the earth is "just another planet"—one where the conditions just happened to be right for life to form and evolve. If there are countless billions of

CREATIONWISE

IT'S MIND BOGGLING TO THINK OF THE VASTNESS OF CREATION! THE BIBLE IS ONLY ONE LITTLE BOOK. JUST THINK OF ALL THE INFORMATION GOD HASN'T GIVEN TO US!

YES, BUT WHAT HAVE YOU DONE WITH THE INFORMATION GOD HAS GIVEN TO US?

© AIG 2003

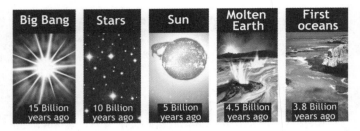

Big Bang	Stars	Sun	Molten Earth	First oceans
15 Billion years ago	10 Billion years ago	5 Billion years ago	4.5 Billion years ago	3.8 Billion years ago

other planets in our galaxy, then surely at least a handful of these worlds have also had the right conditions. Extraterrestrial life is almost inevitable in an evolutionary worldview.

However, the notion of alien life does not square well with Scripture. The earth is unique. God designed the earth for life (Isaiah 45:18). The other planets have an entirely different purpose than does the earth, and thus, they are designed differently. In Genesis 1 we read that God created plants on the earth on Day 3, birds to fly in the atmosphere and marine life to swim in the ocean on Day 5, and animals to inhabit the land on Day 6. Human beings were also made on Day 6 and were given dominion over the animals. But where does the Bible discuss the creation of life on the "lights in the expanse of the heavens"? There is no such description because the lights in the expanse were not designed to accommodate life. God gave care of the earth to man, but the heavens are the Lord's (Psalm 115:16). From a biblical perspective, extraterrestrial life does not seem reasonable.

Problems are multiplied when we consider the possibility of *intelligent* alien life. Science fiction programming abounds with races of people who evolved on other worlds. We see examples of Vulcans and Klingons—pseudohumans similar to us in most respects but different in others. As a plot device, these races allow the exploration of the human condition from the perspective of an outsider. Although very entertaining, such alien races are theologically problematic. Intelligent alien beings cannot be redeemed.

Water covered Earth	Dry land and plants	Sun, moon and stars	Sea and flying creatures	Land animals and man
Day 1-2	Day 3	Day 4	Day 5	Day 6

God's plan of redemption is for human beings: those descended from Adam. Let us examine the conflict between the salvation message and the notion of alien life.

The redemption of mankind

The Bible teaches that the first man, Adam, rebelled against God (Genesis 3). As a result, sin and death entered the world (Romans 5:12). We are all descended from Adam and Eve (Genesis 3:20) and have inherited from them a sin nature (Romans 6:6, 20). This is a problem: sin is a barrier that prevents man from being right with God (Isaiah 59:2). But God loves us despite our sin and provided a plan of redemption—a way to be reconciled with God.

After Adam and Eve sinned, God made coats of skins to cover them (Genesis 3:21). He therefore had to kill at least one animal. This literal action is symbolic of our salvation; an innocent Lamb (Christ—the Lamb of God) would be sacrificed to provide a covering for sin (John 1:29). In the Old Testament, people would sacrifice animals to the Lord as a reminder of their sin (Hebrews 10:3) and as a symbol of the One to come, the Lord Jesus, who would actually pay the penalty for sin.

The animal sacrifices did not actually pay the penalty for sin (Hebrews 10:4, 11). Animals are not related to us; their shed blood cannot count for ours. But the blood of Christ can. Christ is a blood relative of ours since He is descended from Adam as are

we; all human beings are of "one blood" (Acts 17:26). Furthermore, since Christ is also God, His life is of infinite value, and
thus, His death can pay for all the sins of all people. That is why
only the Lord Himself could be our Savior (Isaiah 45:21). Therefore, Christ died once for all (Hebrews 10:10).

The redemption of ET?

When we consider how the salvation plan might apply to any
hypothetical extraterrestrial (but otherwise human-like) beings,
we are presented with a problem. If there were Vulcans or Klingons out there, how would they be saved? They are not blood
relatives of Jesus, and so Christ's shed blood cannot pay for their
sin. One might at first suppose that Christ also visited their world,
lived there, and died there as well, but this is antibiblical. Christ
died *once* for *all* (1 Peter 3:18; Hebrews 9:27–28, 10:10). Jesus is
now and forever both God and man; but He is *not* an alien.

One might suppose that alien beings have never sinned, in
which case they would not need to be redeemed. But then another problem emerges: they suffer the effects of sin, despite having never sinned. Adam's sin has affected all of creation— not
just mankind. Romans 8:20–22 makes it clear that the entirety
of creation suffers under the bondage of corruption. These kinds
of issues highlight the problem of attempting to incorporate an
antibiblical notion into the Christian worldview.

Extraterrestrial life is an evolutionary concept; it does not com-
port with the biblical teachings of the uniqueness of the earth and
the distinct spiritual position of human beings. Of all the worlds
in the universe, it was the earth that God Himself visited, taking
on the additional nature of a human being, dying on a cross, and
rising from the dead in order to redeem all who would trust in
Him. The biblical worldview sharply contrasts with the secular
worldview when it comes to alien life. So, which worldview does
the scientific evidence support? Do modern observations support

the secular notion that the universe is teeming with life, or the biblical notion that earth is unique?

Where is everybody?

So far, no one has discovered life on other planets or detected any radio signals from intelligent aliens. This is certainly what a biblical creationist would expect. Secular astronomers continue to search for life on other worlds, but they have found only rocks and inanimate matter. Their radio searches are met with silence. The real world is the biblical world—a universe designed by God with the earth at the spiritual focal point, not an evolutionary universe teeming with life.

When it comes to extraterrestrial life, science is diametrically opposed to the evolutionary mentality. We currently have *no* evidence of alien life-forms. This problem is not lost on the secular scientists. It has been said that the atomic scientist Enrico Fermi was once discussing the topic of extraterrestrial life when he asked the profound question, "Where is everybody?" Since there are quite possibly multiple billions of planets in our galaxy, and since in the secular view these are all accidents, it is almost inevitable that some of these had the right conditions for life to evolve. And if some of these worlds are billions of years older than ours, then at least some of them would have evolved intelligent life eons ago. The universe should therefore have countless numbers of technologically superior civilizations, any one of which could have colonized our galaxy ages ago. Yet, we find no evidence of these civilizations. Where is everybody? This problem has become known as the "Fermi paradox."

This paradox for evolution is a *feature* of creation. We have seen that the earth is designed for life. With its oceans of liquid water, a protective atmosphere containing abundant free oxygen, and a distance from the sun that is just right for life, earth was certainly designed by God to be inhabited. But the other planets of the universe were not. From the sulfuric acid clouds of Venus to the frozen wasteland of Pluto, the other worlds of our solar system are beautiful and diverse, but they are not designed for life.

What about UFOs?

Sometimes after I speak on the topic of extraterrestrial life, someone will ask me about UFOs. A UFO (unidentified flying object) is just that—an object seen in the sky that is unidentified to the person seeing it. People often want me to explain a sighting of some unknown flying object which they or often a friend have claimed to see. (Sometimes the implication is that if I can't explain it, it somehow proves that it must be an alien spacecraft; but such reasoning is completely vacuous.[1]) These kinds of questions are unreasonable. It is one thing to be asked to interpret evidence that we have, but it is unrealistic to ask someone to interpret un-documented second- or third-hand stories with no actual evidence available for inspection.

There is no doubt that some people sincerely have seen things in the sky that they do not understand. This is hardly surprising since there are lots of things "up there," which can be misunderstood by people not familiar with them. These include Venus, satellites, the international space station, the space shuttle, rockets, Iridium flares, manmade aircraft, internal reflections, meteors, balloons, fireflies, aurorae, birds, ball lightning, lenticular clouds, parhelia, etc. However, a person unfamiliar with these would see a UFO, since the object is "unidentified" to him or her. It is how people interpret what they see that can be questionable.

Remember that we always interpret evidence in light of our worldview. It is therefore crucial to have a correct, biblical worldview. The fallacious worldview of atheism/naturalism may lead someone to draw erroneous conclusions about what they see. From a biblical worldview, we expect to occasionally see things that are not easily explained, since our minds are finite. But UFOs are not alien spacecraft, and of course, there is no tangible evidence to support such a notion.

Why the hype?

In the 1990s the television series *The X-files* entertained millions of fans with stories of aliens, government conspiracies, and one dedicated FBI agent's relentless search for truth. The show's motto, "The truth is out there," is a well-known phrase for sci-fi fans. But why is there such hype surrounding the notion of extraterrestrial life? Why is science fiction programming so popular? Why does SETI spend millions of dollars searching for life in outer space?

The discovery of intelligent extraterrestrial life would certainly be seen as a vindication of evolution; it is an expectation from a naturalistic worldview. But the desire to meet aliens, especially intelligent, technologically advanced ones, seems much more deeply felt than merely to vindicate evolutionary predictions. What is the *real* issue? I've heard a number of different answers from secular astronomers.

In some cases a belief in ETs may stem from a feeling of cosmic loneliness: "If there are aliens, then we would not be alone in the universe." In many cases it comes from an academic desire to learn the mysteries of the universe; a highly developed alien race might have advanced knowledge to pass on to us. Perhaps such knowledge is not merely academic; the hypothetical aliens may know the answers to fundamental questions of existence: "Why am I here? What is the meaning of life?" and so on. An advanced alien race might have medical knowledge far exceeding our own—knowledge which could be used to cure our diseases. Perhaps their medical technology would be so far advanced that they even hold the secret of life and death; with such incredible medical knowledge, perhaps human beings would no longer have to die—*ever*.

In a way, a belief in extraterrestrial life has become a secular replacement for God. God is the one who can heal every disease. God is the one in whom all the treasures of wisdom and knowledge are deposited (Colossians 2:3). God is the one who can answer the fundamental questions of our existence. God alone possesses the gift of eternal life (John 17:3). It is not surprising that the unbelieving scientist would feel a sense of cosmic loneliness, having rejected his Creator. But we are not alone in the universe; there is God. God created us for fellowship with Him; thus, we have an innate need for Him and for purpose. Although human beings have rejected God, in Adam and by our sins as well, our need for fellowship with Him remains.

When I think of the majority of intelligent scientists who have studied God's magnificent creation but have nonetheless rejected Him and have instead chosen to believe in aliens and millions of years of evolution, I am reminded of Romans 1:18–25. God's invisible qualities—His eternal power and divine nature—are clearly revealed in the natural world so that there is no excuse for rejecting God or suppressing the truth about Him. The thinking of man apart from God is nothing more than futile speculations. Exchanging the truth of God, such as creation, for a lie, such as evolution, and turning to a mere creature such as hypothetical aliens for answers is strikingly similar to what is recorded in Romans 1:25.

But when we start from the Bible, the evidence makes sense. The universe is consistent with the biblical teaching that the earth is a special creation. The magnificent beauty and size of a universe, which is apparently devoid of life except for one little world where life abounds, is exactly what we would expect from a biblical worldview. The truth is not "out there;" the truth is *in there*—in the Bible! The Lord Jesus is the truth (John 14:6). So, when we base our thinking on what God has said in His Word, we find that the universe makes sense.

1. The argument is that alien spacecraft could not be explained by a natural phenomenon. Therefore, it is suggested that witnessing something that cannot be explained naturally must prove the existence of alien spacecraft. This is a logical fallacy called "affirming the consequent." It's equivalent to saying, "All white dwarf stars are white. Fred is white; therefore Fred is a white dwarf star."

The Hubble telescope as seen after its last servicing in 2009.
Photo courtesy of NASA.

Viewing the Universe

The universe is so vast that we really can't understand how small we are in comparison. This realization has been incorporated into two very different ways of looking at the meaning of mankind in the universe.

Some have said that with a universe so large and old there must be other civilizations out there. The astronomer Frank Drake developed an equation to estimate the number of civilizations in the Milky Way galaxy that we may be able to communicate with. This equation relies upon the accuracy of evolutionary philosophy. If life cannot come from random arrangement of chemicals, the equation has a probability of zero.

In many science fiction stories, alien life forms are often seen as the saviors of mankind. Mankind is seen as inherently self-destructive or incapable of surviving without the intervention of the visitors. Other versions have the aliens as the creators or designers of life on earth and then returning in various roles. From this position, mankind isn't really special—there are many intelligent civilizations scattered throughout the universe.

The opposite view would be that life is unique to earth, and aliens do not exist. If the emergence of life from nonliving chemicals is not possible, then there are no aliens, ETs, or visitors to speak of. In this view, mankind holds a special position in the universe. Some see this as an arrogant position, but it is the view that is consistent with the Bible.

In the Bible, the earth is the center of the story and the center of God's attention. The Bible makes it clear that mankind did have a Creator but it was not another carbon-based life form. The book of Genesis reveals how God created the universe and then the first man and woman to live in fellowship with Him. Everything was a paradise in the original creation and they were to live forever with no disease, conflict, or war to destroy the race.

The part that the science fiction stories get right is that mankind is capable of great evil. This tendency entered the universe when the first man, Adam, chose to disobey the Creator's rules. Sin entered the world and as a result, the universe now suffers from decay, disease, death, conflict, and suffering. The problem is there are no aliens to save us from ourselves. Left to our own devices, humans are selfish, greedy, manipulative, and deceitful creatures. It might be easy to point the finger at others, but if you stop and truthfully examine your own heart, you'll probably see those qualities within you.

God revealed His commands to mankind through Moses at Mount Sinai. We know these as the Ten Commandments (Exodus 20:1–17). The selfishness, greediness, and deceitfulness that you can find in your own life are offenses against God. You might ask, "Why does God have the right to give me commands?" Since God has created the universe and humans, He has the right to make the rules for His universe. As the Creator, He has revealed that He will punish all of those who reject His commands, just as He punished Adam for his disobedience. If God did not punish those who broke His laws, He would not be just.

> For the wages of sin is death, but the gift of God is eternal life in Christ Jesus our Lord. Romans 6:23

You may think that you have never committed any serious sins against God—you've never murdered or raped anyone—but you may not realize who God is. God defines all that is holy, right, loving, and just. Because He is infinitely holy, a crime against Him warrants an infinite punishment. No matter how many good things you may have done or how much you repaid those you wronged, you cannot pay for the infinite debt you have as a result of your sins against God. Humanity needs someone to save them from this lost state.

Rather than sending aliens to give us some new medicine or technology to save our race, God came to the earth Himself in the person of Jesus Christ. In His mercy, God transported Himself into this physical universe. Jesus lived a life of perfect obedience to God's commands and then chose to suffer on the Cross, bearing the wrath of God against sin.

> But God demonstrates His own love toward us, in that while we were still sinners, Christ died for us. Much more then, having now been justified by His blood, we shall be saved from wrath through Him. For if when we were enemies we were reconciled to God through the death of His Son, much more, having been reconciled, we shall be saved by His life. Romans 5:8–10

Rather than hoping for aliens to save us, we can each have a confident expectation that our sin debt against God has been paid if we will repent of our sins against God and trust that Jesus Christ has paid the penalty for sin on the Cross, rising on the third day to demonstrate His power over death. Confess your sins, turn from them, and ask God to empower you to live your life for Him knowing that Christ has died in your place.

We cannot accomplish our own salvation from the sin in our lives, nor can we expect visitors from another planet to save us. We can, however, have access to a righteousness that does not come from us—an "alien" righteousness from Christ.

In the words of Jesus:

> For God so loved the world that He gave His only begotten Son, that whoever believes in Him should not perish but have everlasting life. For God did not send His Son into the world to condemn the world, but that the

world through Him might be saved. He who believes in Him is not condemned; but he who does not believe is condemned already, because he has not believed in the name of the only begotten Son of God. And this is the condemnation, that the light has come into the world, and men loved darkness rather than light, because their deeds were evil. For everyone practicing evil hates the light and does not come to the light, lest his deeds should be exposed. But he who does the truth comes to the light, that his deeds may be clearly seen, that they have been done in God. John 3:16–21